Sorting

PHOTOGRAPHY
George Siede and Donna Preis

CONSULTANT
Istar Schwager, Ph.D.

Publications
International,
Ltd.

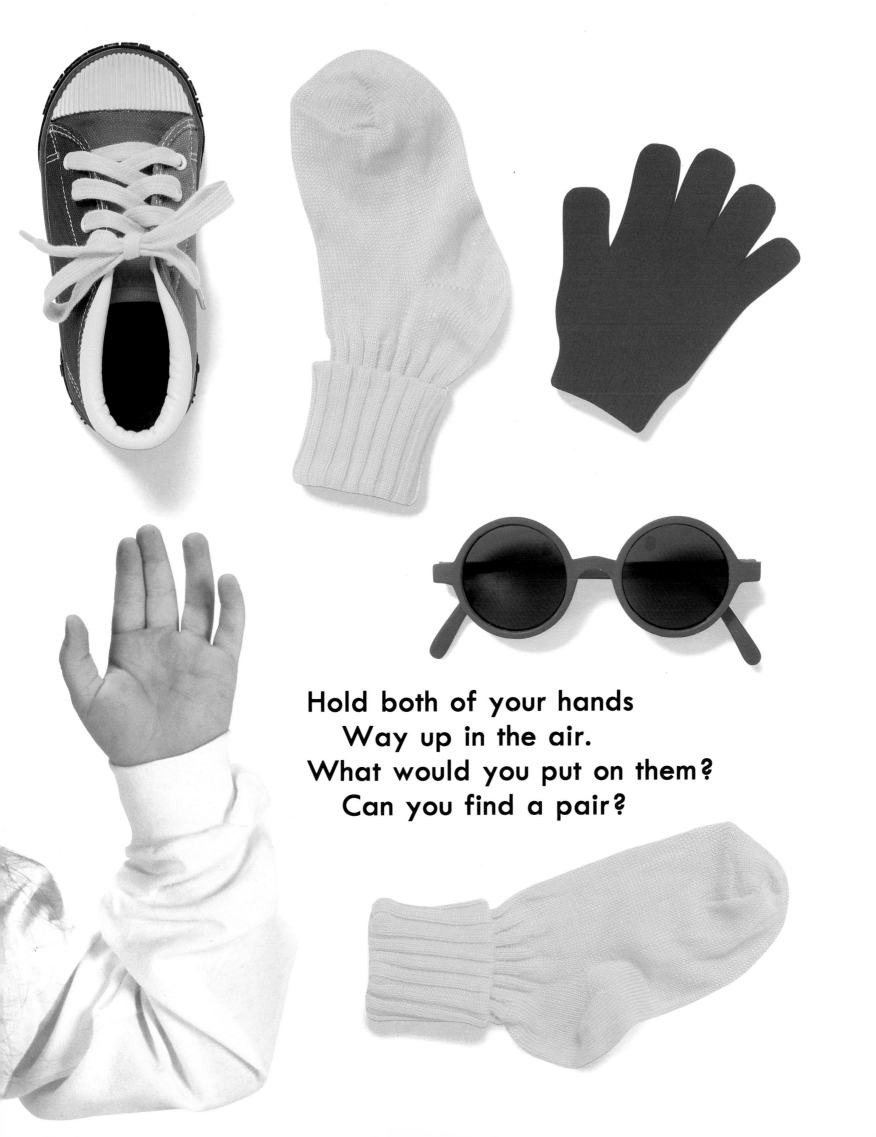

Hold both of your hands
Way up in the air.
What would you put on them?
Can you find a pair?

The big dog likes
   To chase big balls.
The little balls fit
   The little dog's paws.
Which dog wants to play
   With which balls?

This is Rosie.
 She likes red —
Apples, trucks, hats
 For her head.

Point to everything
 that is red.

Sort apples by color;
Help hardworking Fred.
Here's a basket for green
And a basket for red.

Priscilla the Pirate
Says, "Yo-ho-ho!"
Into which chest should
Each treasure go?

Winter days are very cold.
Summer days are very hot.
Can you sort out all this gear?
Can you tell which boy gets what?

Which things are for summer fun?

Which things are for winter fun?

Let's decorate cupcakes;
   Add the finishing touch.
Sprinkle some candies—
   Whoops! Not too much!

What would you never put on a cupcake?

—— Giddy up, cowboy! Get ready to play! ——

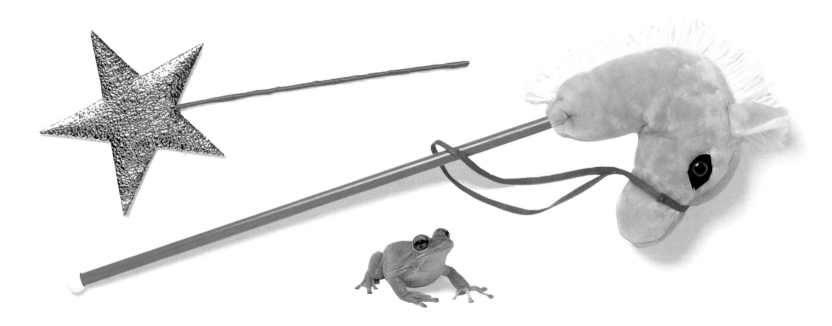

What will Brian pick to play cowboys today? ——

When you grow up,
Which things will you use?

Which scissors?
Which tools?
Which glasses?
Which shoes?

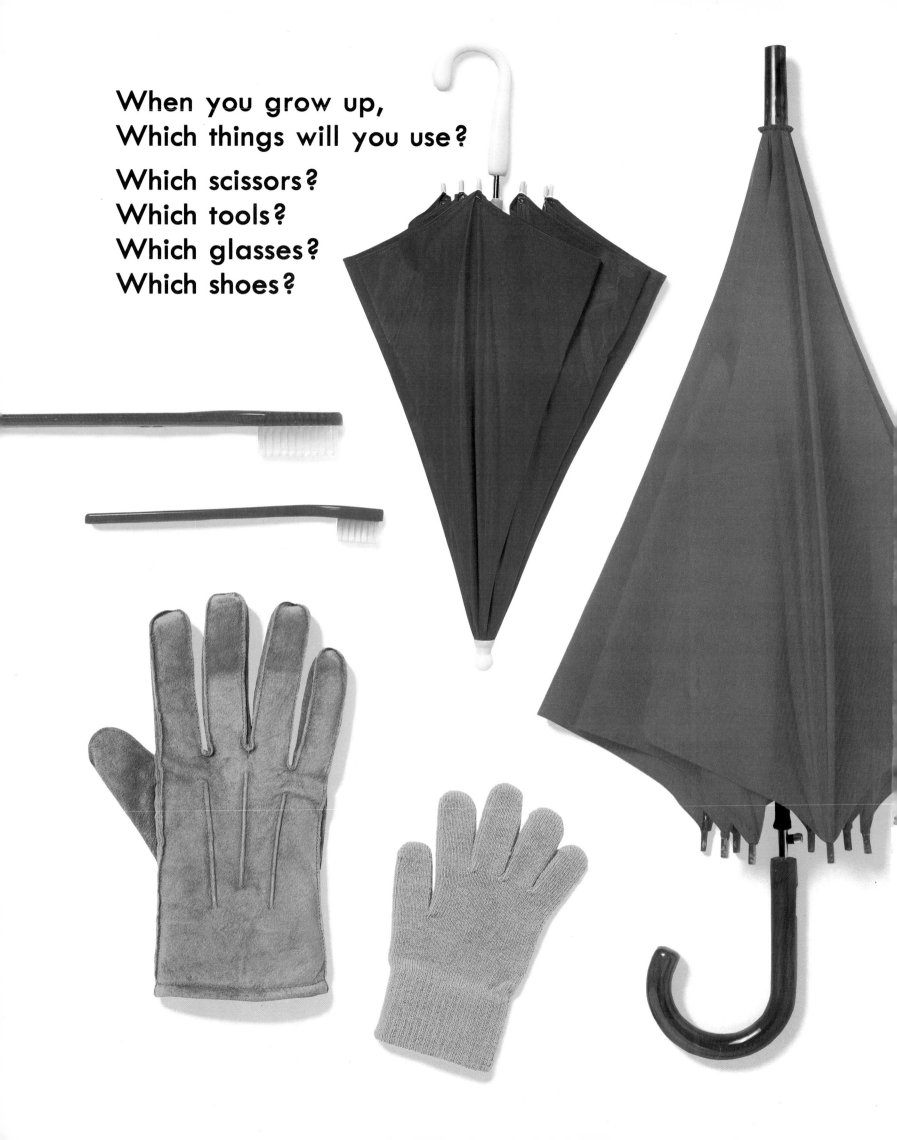

For more fun, take another look

Hold Up Your Hands

How many things are above the girl's head?

When would you wear a warm cap like this one?

Have you ever put your shoes on your hands?

Think up a really good name for this girl.

Dogs at Play

Which dog is the puppy?

The big dog's name is Smiley. Can you guess why?

How many balls have stripes on them?

Could the little dog be the big dog's puppy?

Apple Picking

How many green apples are there?

How many red apples can you count?

Have you ever picked apples from a tree?

Think of something to do with all these apples.

Pirate Treasure

How many square shapes do you see?

How many star shapes do you see?

What would Priscilla use her shovel for?

Do you think Priscilla is a real pirate?

Baking Cupcakes

Find the things that are not for the tops of cupcakes. What are they really for?

How many candles will be on top of your next birthday cake?

Do you see something that is alive? What is it?

Sheriff Brian

How many hats are in this picture?

Have you ever dressed up like a cowboy or cowgirl?

Who would use the magic wand?

Do you know why cowboys and cowgirls wear hats?